Beyond the Gift

*Understanding our God-given Value and
Embracing the Perfecting Love of God*

HOPE RADIANCE BOYD

Beyond the Gift: Understanding our God-given Value and Embracing the Perfecting Love of God.

Copyright © 2025 by Hope Radiance Boyd.

All rights reserved. No part of this book may be reproduced or transmitted in any form or by any means without written permission from the author.

ISBN: 979-8-9921108-4-5

Build A Brother
PUBLISHING

Acknowledgements

To my personal Lord, Savior, King, and Friend. It's in you do I live and move and have my very existence. Thank you for choosing me to be your vessel, and handmaiden. For calling me own. You are mine. Thank you for radically loving me, giving me hope, purpose, and a secured future. I will forever choose you again and again. To serve the Lord and the Kingdom of God is the highest and eternal honor and privilege; to partner with Him to fulfill **His** purposes in the earth as joint heirs with Christ. I am forever indebted.

My dearest family, I love you all so much; each of you have a special place in the chambers of my heart. Thank you for believing in me in times I struggled to believe in myself and what God placed in me. Thank you for standing with me and supporting me naturally and spiritually. I wouldn't trade you all for all tea in China! Let's continue to "Never count God foolish and to make the World our Pulpit." Thanks Daddy. The Best is Yet to come; Heaven is on our side!

To my sister Delki Rosso, moments when I thought I wasn't capable, or felt that my voice wasn't valuable. Thank you for Godly pushing, believing, encouraging, and admonishing me to obey God to write this book. Love you my sister and friend. Lastly, to my dear brother Antonio, thank you for your Godly obedience.

Dedication

To my dear mother, whom I love and miss eternally, the late Dr. Harriet B. Boyd. She was the first woman, and Woman of God, who exemplified humility, grace, and the power of the Holy Ghost to me. Through the echoes of her life, she influenced and taught me to pursue the Lord with all my heart, soul, and might through a personal relationship with Him.

She served the Father as a gracefully broken, surrendered vessel for the Master's use. She was incredibly anointed, gifted, quirky, timeless in her fashion, and sharp in her mind; yet, her deep love for God and His people spoke louder than her works or external influences. I honor her forever for teaching me how to yield to the Holy Spirit, pursue the heart of God, and serve His people with a pure heart and clean hands.

In my heart and spirit, I can still hear her words: "Keep your heart pure, Hope. Keep Jesus at the center, and don't buy the hype." She remains my constant reminder to serve well and love well, starting first by loving and accepting myself as Christ loves and accepts me unconditionally.

I am forever purposed to keep her legacy alive by allowing God to get glory out of my life for the rest of my days.

~ Your Forever Baby

To my Worship and Arts Community and to all Creatives around the world: I pray this book blesses you as it has blessed me. I love you all with the love of Christ. When I say we are insanely creative, anointed, and gifted beyond measure, I mean it. But on the other side of this incredible creativity is the emotional and spiritual weight we often carry—internally and externally, behind closed doors. Many will never know the depth of this burden.

On a blank canvas, the brushstrokes of our pain, victories, and weaknesses somehow form a beautifully broken human masterpiece for the world to see. Yet, with our gifts and talents, we are often used, abused, unseen, and unheard. Sometimes we feel invisible, internally crying out just to be seen, heard, and felt for who we are.

I want you to know this: your value transcends what you do. You are already treasured and loved by your Heavenly Father far beyond what you can ever accomplish or say.

My prayer is that we begin—and continue—to heal, no longer hiding behind the strengths of our gifts and talents. After you've served and poured out to others, you don't have to suffer in silence or navigate your brokenness alone behind closed doors.

I see you. More importantly, God, your Creator, sees you. He loves you deeply. Healing, deliverance, and wholeness are your portion. True freedom—your real value and worth—outshines the stage, the podium, the garment, the song, and the lights.

The Father desires you to experience His freedom, healing, and love in every area of your life. You are more than your gifts and abilities. You are a precious son or daughter of the Most High God.

Creatives, my friends, **let's be made whole in Jesus' name.**

Table of Contents

Letter 1 | I'm Not Enough 8

Letter 2 | Our Gifts/Talents Don't Save Us 18

Letter 3 | Keep Your Heart Pure: The Two-Edged Sword 26

Letter 4 | My Thorn Is My Salvation 36

Letter 5 | My Creativity Is Powered By Elohim 44

Letter 6 | The Value Of The One | Parable Of The Talents 54

Letter 7 | Identity: I Am | The Higher Calling To Sonship 60

Letter 8| "I Am" Embodied Rhema Declaration 69

Letter 9 | "I Ascend" Embodied Rhema Declaration 73

Letter 10 | "Be Healed" 77

About The Author 81

LETTER 1 | I'M NOT ENOUGH

LETTER 1 | I'M NOT ENOUGH

Who am I without my gifts, my talents, my works? Who would know me? Would anyone accept or love me for who I am outside of what I do? Am I enough beyond my gifts, talents, title, my works?

What if I told you that everything you are looking for outside of yourself... God already placed it there—inside of you. Trapped, waiting for you to realize who you are. Your "enough" isn't defined by what you do; it's who you are as a daughter or son of the Most High God. Your "enough" isn't defined by what you can produce as a creative, artist, leader, or believer.

The gospel artist Darrel Walls said it best: "We are not our gifts; we just have them." I'll tell you this: your "enough" is defined by your identity in Christ and what Abba Father says about you.

FLASHBACK| Years ago, while grieving the passing of my mother, the late Dr. Harriet B. Boyd, I was in a state of functioning depression and grief, yet still actively teaching, ministering around the world, serving, and pouring out with a bleeding heart. There were times after ministering when I would just cry. I was avoiding dealing with where I was emotionally and mentally. One day, while cleaning my kitchen in my apartment, I heard the Holy Spirit say, "I can't heal what you don't reveal."

Gifts and callings are without repentance. After the Lord would use me to minister across cities and nations, I would go home to crippling fear, depression, and anxiety that would suffocate me. It isn't the Lord's will for His people to be bound. It is not His will for us to declare the works of the Lord—healing, breakthrough, and deliverance for others—while we deny the SAME Spirit that came to set us free. That is sin; it's unbelief.

2 Timothy 3:5 says, *"Having a form of godliness, but denying the power thereof: from such turn away."* The Lord desires truth in the inward parts; He desires His children to be made whole behind closed doors and beyond our gifts.

3 John 1:2

"Beloved, I pray that you may prosper in all things and be in health, just as your soul prospers."

In order for wholeness to take place, we must identify the root of the "why" of our brokenness by exposing the pain, disappointment, words that were spoken, and/or past experiences that we may consciously or unconsciously rehearse to ourselves. By inviting the Holy Spirit into those intimate, dark spaces and asking Him to shine the light of His love to reveal and lay bare our fears, insecurities, and inadequacies that are hidden in our soul, we can begin to heal. This is critical to loosening the stronghold of the enemy in our minds. The enemy loves secrecy and isolation, but there is power in our confession!

Proverbs 28:13

"Whoever conceals their sins does not prosper, but the one who confesses and renounces them finds mercy."

We must present our hearts on display for the Holy Spirit to search and find us right where we are.

True freedom comes beyond the audience, stage, lights, and people; it's in the presence of the true and living God. Our gifts, talents, or works will only take us so far in providing "false security." We can't mask confidence, healing, and our worth with a gift or talent or by our works. Trust me, I've tried. Healing, freedom, and confidence are a sound. They are a vibration, a spirit that will echo through the pages of your life—spiritually and naturally.

There's no amount of praise, accolades, or affirmations about what you do or your gift that can fill that void inside. We will begin to seek and yearn for acceptance and validation in the praises of man. We will look to man to tell us or make us feel that we are valued and "enough" when God Himself has already told us who we are and whose we are.

John 1:12

"But as many as received Him, to them He gave the right to become children of God, even to those who believe in His name."

If we don't come to Abba Father with our weaknesses, brokenness, or dysfunctions, they'll infiltrate our gifts, how we serve others, and how we treat ourselves. Our natural and spiritual lives are yoked together.

CASE IN POINT | If, throughout life, you never felt accepted in your family or certain spaces, you might have done works to gain approval or to be loved. You might have felt like you had to earn affection, acceptance, and love from loved ones or others based on what you did rather than for who you are. You might have felt like you had to prove yourself, but nothing ever seemed enough. This undealt-with experience in the natural could transfer into your relationship with God and with others. You might feel that, in order for God to use you, receive you, or love you, it's earned by your works or by doing everything "right," like an earning system.

In relationships, you may start to people-please and chase after others' affirmation, validation, and acceptance. When they don't give you what you were internally hoping for, you turn that pain inward, questioning yourself: "What did I do wrong?" or "What's wrong with me?"

To be honest, we can unknowingly place unrealistic expectations and standards on ourselves due to our own internal fears and insecurities. These can morph into perfectionism, which is a form of unhealthy pride. Perfectionism unchecked will make you feel that whatever you do isn't "enough." You run after and obsess over the next moment or next high of success or external gain to fill a sense of wholeness. But unchecked perfectionism only leads to temporary satisfaction.

If this is you (because this was me), you are worthy and enough whether you produce something or not in the public eye. You are not measured by the opinions of people or by what you do. You are measured by the immeasurable love of God. There's a part of us, as humans, that must continually let go of the spirit of pride: the pride of not wanting to be wrong or corrected and the pride of wanting to appear unblemished before the eyes of man while internally self-destructing.

Surrender the spirit of pride today so that the Lord can take out the stony heart and give you a heart of flesh, so the Holy Spirit can do a perfect work of healing in you. Be free from self-bondage in Jesus' name. Be kind to yourself, give yourself permission to grow in His grace, embrace your humanity, and accept yourself as Christ does. Your abilities and works don't define you.

I'm here to tell you: the devil is a liar. You are more than enough and loved because God, your Heavenly Father, first loved you and chose you. Our validation, worth, and value are already written. It is finished.

1 John 4:19

"We love because he first loved us."

Romans 5:8-9

"But God shows his love for us in that while we were still sinners, Christ died for us. Since, therefore, we have now been justified by his blood, much more shall we be saved by him from the wrath of God."

You are not alone.

Moses and Gideon, to name a few, were some of the greatest in the Hall of Faith in the Bible. Even they felt insecure, filled with self-doubt, and plagued by inadequacies. Another example: God commanded Joshua to "Be not afraid" multiple times in Joshua 1. God knows the internal fractures in His sons and daughters. And guess what? It doesn't make Him love you any less or make you unusable. God had to affirm and validate His servant leaders countless times in the Bible. In the same breath, "I AM THAT I AM" (Exodus 3:14), the

LETTER 1 | I'M NOT ENOUGH

LORD who is the self-sufficient One, validates and affirms you through His Word—even in your weakness.

Again, I ask you: Who are you without your gift, talent, or title? I'll tell you who you are… You are a child of the Most High God. [Put your "spiritual" crown on.]

1 Peter 2:9

"You are a chosen people, a royal priesthood, a holy nation, God's special possession, that you may declare the praises of Him who called you out of darkness into His wonderful light."

You are joint heirs with Christ Jesus. YOU ARE MORE THAN ENOUGH. WELL, MORE THAN ABLE. We have the God of Abraham, Isaac, and Jacob living on the inside of us. Nothing—I mean NOTHING—lacks in Him. So, YOU lack nothing in Him. YOU ARE ENOUGH. But in order for this identity to become RHEMA—alive and active in your mind, heart, and spirit—we **must** come to God with radical transparency and honesty so He can remove the spiritual veils of pain, deception, offense, disappointment…whatever it is.

Hebrews 4:16

"Let us then approach God's throne of grace with confidence, so that we may receive mercy and find grace to help us in our time of need."

1 John 1:9

"If we confess our sins, He is faithful and just and will forgive us our sins and purify us from all unrighteousness."

Through prayer and divine revelation from the Holy Spirit, we must uproot and renounce word curses, childhood or past experiences, and false narratives that cause brokenness in our souls. Whether we consciously or subconsciously believed those lies, we must surrender them to God. Once revealed, uprooted, renounced, and surrendered, we must replace the pain and trauma with the power of God's Word and go through the process of healing daily. Healing is the children's bread. Healing and wholeness belong to us, but it is also our personal responsibility. The Holy Spirit is our helper and partner in this journey. Believer, BE HEALED in Jesus' name.

The reality is this: the gravity of your healing and deliverance goes beyond your gifts and talents. It is way bigger than you. You have an adversary, the ruler of the Kingdom of Darkness, Satan, who is assigned to obstruct your destiny and freedom in Christ.

1 Peter 5:8

"Be sober, be vigilant; because your adversary the devil, as a roaring lion, walketh about, seeking whom he may devour."

Notice it says "as a roaring lion"—a simile comparing something to what it isn't. It's essentially a mirage. This reminds me of the nostalgic movie "The Wizard of Oz." Side note: my mother despised that movie; it frightened her even as a little girl. She would skip past it without hesitation whenever it came on TV. Anyway, in the movie, the Wizard appeared to be a powerful, intimidating ruler. He bullied the main characters, who were plagued with fear, lack of courage, and insecurity. However, by the end of the movie, the characters overcame their inadequacies and discovered the Wizard was just an old man with no real power.

Spiritually, the enemy doesn't have as much power as he portrays. However, he is cunning, observant, and a strategist. He preys on our vulnerabilities, observing patterns and weaknesses from childhood. But his power is only what we give or relinquish to him. While he is the accuser of the brethren and the father of lies, Satan must ask permission to test and try us. The enemy can only sway us through the unhealed gates we have not yet surrendered to God. But there is a greater power working within us that triumphs over the enemy in our minds, situations, and destiny.

1 John 4:4

"You are of God, little children, and have overcome them, because He who is in you is greater than he who is in the world."

LETTER 1 | I'M NOT ENOUGH

The Father has come that we may have life and have it more abundantly. But "The thief comes only to steal, kill, and destroy"—joy, esteem, identity, and destiny—to keep veils of deception, blindness, and pain over our eyes so we never tap into the fullness of our God-identity. The weapon the enemy uses is often YOU. The enemy cannot infiltrate what we don't give him access to. We must put on the full armor of God!

Ephesians 6:10-18

"Finally, be strong in the Lord and in His mighty power. Put on the full armor of God so that you can take your stand against the devil's schemes. For our struggle is not against flesh and blood, but against the rulers, authorities, powers of this dark world, and spiritual forces of evil in the heavenly realms. Therefore, put on the full armor of God so that when the day of evil comes, you may stand your ground. And after you have done everything, to stand. Stand firm then, with the belt of truth buckled around your waist, with the breastplate of righteousness in place, and with your feet fitted with the readiness from the gospel of peace. In addition, take up the shield of faith, with which you can extinguish all the flaming arrows of the evil one. Take the helmet of salvation and the sword of the Spirit, which is the Word of God. And pray in the Spirit on all occasions with all kinds of prayers and requests. With this in mind, be alert and always keep on praying for all the Lord's people."

We must invite the Holy Spirit to reveal and heal unhealed gates through prayer, fasting, honesty, and accountability, doing the work of inner healing and deliverance daily. Be encouraged! Here is your reality: You are already made in the image of Christ. Your worth is already settled in Him. Your value is priceless! You are incomparable. This truth was settled at Calvary when He died for you and me.

By recognizing that we are valued beyond our works, we can engage with the world more freely, serving and loving others from a place of wholeness. The focus on inner transformation and emotional healing speaks to the deep need for authenticity in our original design, reminding us that true fulfillment comes from embracing our inherent worth from our Heavenly Father. Value the thoughts God has toward you—that is your identity. They are higher, they are full of unfailing hope and promises, and they are true. BELIEVE IT!

Isaiah 55:8-9

"For my thoughts are not your thoughts, neither are your ways my ways," declares the Lord. "As the heavens are higher than the earth, so are my ways higher than your ways and my thoughts than your thoughts."

LETTER 1 | I'M NOT ENOUGH

SELF REFLECTION

LETTER 2 | OUR GIFTS/TALENTS DON'T SAVE US

LETTER 2 | OUR GIFTS/TALENTS DON'T SAVE US

It's easy to hide behind our strengths; it takes courage to expose and lean into being made whole in our brokenness. There is a difference between brokenness and weaknesses. Weakness deals with the thorn in our flesh, like Paul's, that God will place and sometimes keep there to help us remain humble and always running to Him as our source. For clarity, I'm not speaking about brokenness in spirit (Psalms 51:17). I'm addressing the brokenness within the soul—unhealed, undealt-with gates that need deliverance, soul tears (emotional wounds, traumas, anger, etc.).

The gift or talent is a gift that God has given us to use for His purpose and for His glory. The gift is there as a vehicle or a drawing card to point people back to Christ, to fulfill purposes and assignments on earth, in the lives of others. In return, the gifts and talents will make room, open doors for us, and bring us before great men for His glory to shine through.

God has placed a gift or talent in every single person that will allow us to fulfill His vision and purpose on earth. However, our gift isn't all-encompassing to save us or deliver us. The gift or talent cannot substitute our healing, deliverance, and relationship with the Lord. The gift is a service; it's not who you are.

CONTEXT QUESTION So, if we aren't performing or doing, are we not still saved, delivered, or committed to our relationship with Father God? The only true deliverer and savior is Jesus Christ. I've heard creatives say (and I've said it myself), "If I didn't have dance or singing, etc., in my life, I would have died or I don't know where I would be." That's correct to an extent. Nonetheless, the gift is the resource or the tool that God used, but it wasn't the source of my healing, salvation, or deliverance. It was GOD.

THINK ABOUT IT Famous celebrities with status, money, exposure, their talents, access to countless materialistic things, and relationships—surprisingly, these aren't enough to fill them or make them whole. There's always a void. The spirit of depression and despair, resulting in hopelessness and even suicide, is at an all-time high, even among youth, young adults, leaders, and pastors.

FLASHBACK The pandemic in 2020 was a hard year for many people. Many youth, young adults, creatives, pastors, artists, leaders, and movers were oppressed with manic depression, suicidal thoughts, separation anxiety, and questioning their identity. They felt, "Who am I without using my gift/talent or works?" We were so used to being on the go, go, go; now we were forced to be still... still... still. We somehow attached our identity to our works. We had to face it. We had to face ourselves, our raw thoughts, and the dysfunctions we had been running from or avoiding. But I can tell you this—the stillness was intentional.

Psalm 62:5

"For God alone, O my soul, wait in silence, for my hope is from Him."

The Holy Spirit told me while I was crying out to Him one night, "I am in the stillness; I am in the isolation." It was in the stillness and silence where God affirmed me, corrected me, aligned me, started the healing journey in me, and revealed my value and identity in Him. He told me He loved me beyond my works. It is who I am as His daughter, His handmaiden, and His friend. "My value is already settled" (thanks, Ellie).

TRANSPARENCY MOMENT I used to pray in tears, "LORD, show me who 'Hope' is through Your eyes so I can see myself the way You do!" For years, I prayed this prayer until one day, in a still small voice, the Holy Spirit said, "I already did. It's in My Word." I wiped the tears off my face and opened the Word of God. I still chuckle at this moment

LETTER 2 | OUR GIFTS/TALENTS DON'T SAVE US

because every affirmation and validation we yearn for outside of ourselves from imperfect people, God has already given us in His Word.

TRUTH IS We won't know our value, Christ-identity, and God-given birthrights if we don't open the Blueprint—the Word of God—daily. Everything in His Word will dispel every lie from the enemy and radiate His truth in our souls.

SELF-REFLECTION After you perform, minister, or serve others, when the high is gone and you are back in solitude, do you still feel an emptiness or longing to perform to feel a sense of gratification?

Gifts and callings are without repentance. As a creative and servant leader for over 10 years, I know that we can do what we do in our sleep. It's effortless because God anoints us; He gives us the ability. The gift is a gift—whether you're saved or unsaved. The key is how we use or interpret the value and purpose of the gift that matters. The gift or talent cannot become our identity.

FLASHBACK I remember battling crippling fear and anxiety in my mind due to undealt-with emotional gates of fear, loss, and abandonment. I would host conferences, productions, and events, and the Holy Spirit was present. People were saved, delivered, and transformed. But I would go home to tormenting spirits. I see how people can cross over into mental illnesses. It wasn't until I realized that gifts or works can't replace the continual process of inner healing, deliverance, and relationship with God.

Yes, God will still use you at His discretion. But why would it be God's will for us to "save the whole world" and become castaways?

1 Corinthians 9:27

"But I discipline my body and bring it into subjection, lest when I have preached to others, I myself should become disqualified [castaway]."

Are you willing to disqualify your own healing and breakthrough to become a castaway to the very thing you proclaimed and believed for others but didn't believe for yourself? THE DEVIL IS A LIAR.

You are worthy to be healed. You are worthy to be set free. And guess what? You are already free in Jesus' name. Walk out the process. You don't have to stay where you are. You don't have to hide behind your gift, talent, or works to feel valued, loved, or enough. You have significance beyond your works. It's hidden, wrapped up in Christ.

John 8:36

"So if the Son makes you free, then you are unquestionably free."

Romans 5:8

"But God demonstrates His own love for us in this: While we were still sinners, Christ died for us."

Your wholeness, healing, and value are already paid in FULL. Walk in it! We don't earn God's love; His love isn't transactional. It's unconditional because He first loved us. We don't have to make our gift and works an idol out of fear that we have no worth or relevance without them. Let's put the gift, talent, and works in the right place in our hearts.

TRANSPARENCY MOMENT I thought if I wasn't consistently doing for the Lord, I wasn't significant. I felt I had to earn love or affirmation from God or man. But God has already affirmed me beyond my gifts and works. God is not like man. Truth is, God wants intimate communion and fellowship more than our works anyway. That's true relationship; true sonship with Father God.

THINK ABOUT IT Jesus placed more priority on prayer and communion with His Heavenly Father. Jesus was in such oneness with Him that miracles took only seconds or moments. Relationship over works.

LETTER 2 | OUR GIFTS/TALENTS DON'T SAVE US

SELF-REFLECTION As we do ministry, teaching, or performing, are we working for the Father or with the Father? There's a big difference. We can't be so busy doing things for God that we forget to simply BE with Him. Ouch. I felt that too.

The Father desires the spirit of sonship in His sons and daughters. Sonship is about relationship with Abba Father more than works, performance, or ministry. Again, creative, friend, believer, I pose the question: Who are you beyond the gift or talent? Who are you beyond your works or performance? I'll tell you who you are again: You are a child of God. You are chosen. You are valued. You are His masterpiece and treasured possession.

RANDOM THOUGHT CONNECTION When people retire or experience empty nest syndrome, they often fall into depression because they have tied their identity to their works, title, or serving others. We cannot make the mistake of tying our identity to what we do or attaching our identity to people. Unconsciously, we become slaves to our works or title and not to God. When He tells us to shift in situations and relationships, we wrestle with it because we've made it an idol in our hearts. I know it's comfortable and familiar, but God often disrupts our patterns to create uncomfortable situations to encourage, chastise, and redirect us.

Proverbs 19:21

"Many are the plans in a person's heart, but it is the Lord's purpose that prevails."

Obedience isn't always easy, but it is profitable. Let's yield to the signs, instructions, and obey. Know that your gifts and talents don't save you. They can't replace healing, deliverance in the soul, and relationship with your Heavenly Father. Our gifts are valuable and needed on earth, and yes, we need to fulfill what He has called us to do. But they are not who we are. You are a child of God, and the Father deeply loves you. He wants you. He yearns for you. Not the gift part of you—just YOU.

1 John 3:1

"See what kind of love the Father has given to us, that we should be called children of God; and so we are."

Communion: It's in those times of fellowship with the Holy Spirit where He ministers to our souls and minds. He reveals and uncovers gates of personal brokenness, weaknesses, and underlying heart matters. He heals us, corrects us, aligns our hearts with His, and makes us whole.

Jeremiah 31:1

"The Lord appeared to him from far away. I have loved you with an everlasting love; therefore, I have continued my faithfulness to you."

LETTER 2 | OUR GIFTS/TALENTS DON'T SAVE US

SELF REFLECTION

LETTER 3 | KEEP YOUR HEART PURE: THE TWO-EDGED SWORD

LETTER 3 | KEEP YOUR HEART PURE: THE TWO-EDGED SWORD

Matthew 5:8

"Blessed are the pure in heart, for they will see God."

My mother, who has gone on to be with the Lord, married this scripture in her heart and spirit and lived this testament until her last days. She would always admonish me, my sisters, my brother, and the untold lives she impacted around the world to "Keep your heart pure." To this day, this mantra resounds as a standard in my life. As I got older, this scriptural phrase has been sweet but also tried in the fire, tested, and proven. It has transcended from just a saying to a lifestyle, a heart's posture that's on continual display: "The pure in heart, for they will see God."

The Holy Spirit illuminated to me that "to see God" means to see Him in all things through His eyes—to see ourselves, people, and circumstances through His eyes. The eyes are the perspective of the heart. The eyes are the lenses, the mind is the processor, the heart is the storage and filter, and the mouth is the interpreter. We can't see God in all things when there is no filter (or sifter) on the eyes of the heart. The heart affects the eyes, the eyes affect the mind, and the mind affects the mouth. Your hands and mouth are connected to your heart. It may seem like a lot, but stay with me; I'm going somewhere with this.

Luke 6:45

"A good man brings good things out of the good stored up in his heart, and an evil man brings evil things out of the evil stored up in his heart. For the mouth speaks what the heart is full of."

Love Thy Enemies

We are admonished to love and pray for our enemies, and we must forgive even if we did nothing wrong. Here's the thing: in our human nature, we don't know how to love with a Christ-like love. We must ask for this type of love, and the Holy Spirit must teach us how to love like Him. When we operate in agape love, the intent of our hearts and love will be tested and perfected by God.

The pure in heart is a two-edged sword. God commands us in Matthew 5:43-48:

"You have heard that it was said, 'Love your neighbor and hate your enemy.' But I tell you, love your enemies and pray for those who persecute you, that you may be children of your Father in heaven. He causes His sun to rise on the evil and the good and sends rain on the righteous and the unrighteous. If you love only those who love you, what reward do you have? And if you greet only your brothers, what more than others are you doing? Be perfect [growing into spiritual maturity both in mind and character, actively integrating godly values into your daily life], as your heavenly Father is perfect."

Through this text, God wants to perfect our love walk. It's not just about the person; it's about our obedience to Him. We must strive daily, through the help of the Holy Spirit, to embody the scripture that says, "To love your neighbor as you love yourself." But if we struggle with loving our imperfectly perfect selves, we will struggle to love others the way God loves us. We aren't responsible for someone else's response, but only for ours. God is all about relationship. How you treat and handle others is a reflection of yourself; it's a mirror.

Proverbs 27:19

"As in water face reflects face, so a man's heart reveals the man."

TRUTH IS

It is not easy to love with agape love without the Holy Spirit. It's one of the fruits of the Spirit that we must possess (Galatians 5:22-23).

LETTER 3 | KEEP YOUR HEART PURE: THE TWO-EDGED SWORD

When we learn to love our enemy, it reflects the Spirit of love working within our hearts and lives. When we choose to love, we allow the Holy Spirit to work on our character and integrity and perfect our love. Anyone can love someone who loves them; that's easy. To love all people the way Christ loves us? Ouu Jesus... that can be painful to our flesh. Yet it reveals our motives—how and why we love—and this will translate into how we demonstrate our service to God and others.

SELF-REFLECTION

- Do you love God, yourself, and others conditionally or unconditionally?
- Do you love God and people based on what you can gain from it? Is it transactional love?
- Are you serving people or wanting people to serve you for validation or acceptance?

I'm speaking heavily on this because this is what God has confronted me with, delivered me from, and is still delivering me from by His grace.

Side note: Just because God has delivered us from some things, we must still stay sober, vigilant, and humble.

FLASHBACK There was a time in my life when I allowed people to use and abuse my gifts and talents. At times, I didn't even realize I was being used. But on the contrary, there were times I knew with my eyes wide open what was going on. Because I have a heartbeat for collaboration, unity, and serving others genuinely, this kind of heart can easily be taken advantage of by people with ulterior motives or opportunistic spirits. I would serve others, and in my heart of hearts, I served with pure intentions. However, wisdom and maturity now tell me, "Every opportunity and every connection isn't a God door or a God connection," even with good intentions. We must pray and use spiritual discernment to understand what God truly wants for us, rather than mixing in our own human desires, compassion, and hidden ambitions.

BACK TO THE POINT Unconsciously and consciously being used for my gifting, I pressed on to love and serve because I believed that even though I was brought into these spaces with ulterior motives, God could still get the glory out of why I was sent there. There were times when, after ministering or serving while knowing I was being used for my gift, they would smile with me in the moment. But after the gift served its purpose, they all went away. There was a moment when I bawled my eyes out in the bathroom stall, feeling so used. I couldn't wrap my mind around the why—why they couldn't receive me, accept me, or value me outside of my gift.

I believe this was the moment God told me enough was enough of "casting my pearls before swine" (Matthew 7:6-7). In these growth and maturing pains, I've learned how to put value back on myself. It's okay to say no without feeling a sense of guilt or fear behind it. People who understand and value your heart, and all in all have pure motives concerning you, will love you and treat you righteously whether you do or don't. These experiences in my life were allowed by God so He could deal with and minister to a deeper issue beyond people. He uncovered my need for validation and acceptance from others. Why did I need or seek their validation and acceptance? God ministered to that part of me, and I found healing and deliverance.

I'm telling you, your love walk with the Holy Spirit is a two-edged sword. People will only do to you what YOU allow. But the loaded question is not WHAT they are doing; it's WHY you ALLOW it. And when you know the why, deliverance and freedom are there for you. Once Abba showed me my heart, He revealed in part to me the person's heart issue and the why behind their actions. It had NOTHING to do with me or others; it was a spirit.

Father revealed this to me not for me to judge or have a one-up attitude. He disclosed it so I would PRAY and INTERCEDE for their hearts. This experience was purposed to perfect my heart, teaching me how to LOVE as Christ loves me. I have also seen, through obedience in love, that the Lord will make your enemies be at peace with you and even use those same people to bless you!

LETTER 3 | KEEP YOUR HEART PURE: THE TWO-EDGED SWORD

Side note: How can God prepare a table for you in the presence of your enemies or make your enemy your footstool if you're cutting off and exposing everybody? Most times, God will allow you to discern spirits to give you the wisdom to navigate relationships, putting them in the right place. This takes spiritual and emotional maturity; it can open doors for you, or the lack thereof can hinder and close them.

Ephesians 6:12

"For our struggle is not against flesh and blood, but against the rulers, against the authorities, against the powers of this dark world, and against the spiritual forces of evil in the heavenly realms."

Unfiltered Hearts Our hearts are filters. Just as in the natural, where AC air filters need regular renewal in our homes, the filters of our hearts must also be renewed frequently. Clogged, unclean filters can have physical and internal effects on an environment and the body. They can cause impurities in the air (pollution), lead to bacteria growth, and affect air quality. Internally, they may cause headaches, fatigue, tightness in the chest, and other symptoms that are difficult to shake. It's imperative to change filters regularly.

Spiritually, unclean hearts mirror these effects. Impurities stored in the heart will cause our words to filter out spiritual and emotional pollution—hurt, offense, and pain—that will affect those around us. An impure heart can cloud your perspective and how you see yourself, God, your situation, and others. Purity of the heart leads to clarity in the spirit and the natural. An unfiltered heart carrying emotional weight can even cause internal physical health issues, like stress and tension, that manifest as illnesses in the physical body.

Proverbs 4:23

"Guard your heart with all diligence [above all else], for it determines the course of your life."

FLASHBACK

I remember a time when a seed of bitterness tried to take root in my heart. It began with disappointment from someone dear to me, and instead of dealing with it internally, my heart began to turn. That bitterness grew—first in my heart, then into my words, which became laced with negativity and resentment. Finally, my actions reflected the pain hidden within.

Listen, the enemy often uses what is closest to us to bind us. That situation began to change me into someone I didn't want to be—someone I wasn't. The weight of unforgiveness, offense, grief, and pain is too heavy to carry. We cannot allow the burdens of the heart to affect our present or future. Scripture reminds us to "guard our hearts with all diligence" and to "strip off every weight that slows us down, especially the sin that so easily trips us up" (Hebrews 12:1-3). Part of this process involves having boundaries. As Ephesians 4:26 says, "Be angry, but do not sin." Honor your feelings and be honest about them, but don't dwell on those emotions. When left unchecked, they take root and grow.

BACK TO THE STORY

I thank God for the Holy Spirit. When He is present in our lives, darkness cannot remain. Light drives out darkness.

John 1:5:

"The light shines in the darkness, and the darkness has not overcome it."

One night, the Holy Spirit revealed the bitterness and hurt in my heart. As I spoke, I could hear it in my voice. He showed me the condition of my heart, and I was instantly convicted. I repented, prayed, and asked Him to help me let go. I chose to forgive. It hurt, but I knew I couldn't allow it to affect my relationship with God.

LETTER 3 | KEEP YOUR HEART PURE: THE TWO-EDGED SWORD

Matthew 6:14:

"For if you forgive other people when they sin against you, your heavenly Father will also forgive you."

We must let go of unforgiveness and offense—forces that fester deep within the Body of Christ, creatives, and believers. The enemy thrives on confusion and division. Let's reject the spirit of pride. When we serve with bitterness, we lay a dirty gift at the altar, offering it with unclean hands.

Matthew 5:23-24:

"If you are offering your gift at the altar and there remember that your brother or sister has something against you, leave your gift there in front of the altar. First go and be reconciled to them; then come and offer your gift."

TRUTH IS

Letting go of pain and situations that bind us is one of the most difficult but freeing choices we can make. In time, you will thank God for the decision to forgive.

1 John 1:7:

"But if we walk in the light, as He is in the light, we have fellowship with one another, and the blood of Jesus, His Son, cleanses us from all sin."

My constant prayer is this:

Lord, may I never give people or situations such power over me that it blocks or taints my heart, hands, and blessings. A pure heart and spirit are the key to everything in life, for out of them flow the issues of life.

LOVE BEYOND THE GIFT

The story of the prodigal son reminds me of God's heart. When the elder brother refused to celebrate his younger sibling's return, his father said, "You are always with me, and everything I have is yours" (Luke 15:31). This parable reveals both the Father's redemptive power and our tendency toward self-righteousness.

We must not serve God based on works alone while neglecting love. Agape love transforms everything. It is the foundation of our relationship with God and with others. Love is not transactional or hierarchical. It is resolute, and it flows from a heart surrendered to God.

1 Corinthians 13:1-3:

"If I speak in the tongues of men or of angels, but do not have love, I am only a resounding gong or a clanging cymbal. If I have the gift of prophecy and can fathom all mysteries and all knowledge, but do not have love, I am nothing."

Gifts and callings are without repentance, but love is the essence that gives them meaning. Without love, our works and gifts are nothing.

REFLECTION

Ask yourself:

- What is the motive behind my service?
- Why do I obey the Lord?

Love is a reflection of the heart. It cannot be masked or faked. God's love transforms us, shaping our actions and how we serve Him and others.

Philippians 1:9-11:

"So this is my prayer: that your love may abound more and more in knowledge and depth of insight, so that you may be able to discern what is best and may be pure and blameless for the day of Christ."

LETTER 3 | KEEP YOUR HEART PURE: THE TWO-EDGED SWORD

MY CONSTANT PRAYER

Father, search my heart. Reveal anything that is not like **You**. Uproot it and help me to be delivered through Your Word. Teach me to love as You do. Help me serve with pure hands and a pure heart, not out of duty but out of love for You. Mold me, correct me, and align me with Your heart. Amen.

LETTER 4 | MY THORN IS MY SALVATION

LETTER 4 | MY THORN IS MY SALVATION

2 Corinthians 12:9

"My grace is sufficient for you, for my power is made perfect in weakness." Therefore, I will boast all the more gladly about my weaknesses, so that Christ's power may rest on me."

Being weak freed me.

My weakness became my superpower.

Isaiah 40:29

"He gives power to the weak, and to those who have no might He increases strength."

For a long time, I lived in the mindset of perfection. I believed that doing everything "right" in the sight of God made me righteous. I thought my righteousness was rooted in my ability to avoid mistakes, to live without error. I assumed God would use me more if I didn't "physically sin."

But the truth is, whether sin is visible or hidden, it's still sin. The Holy Spirit revealed to me that sins of the heart and sins of the tongue are just as grievous as the external acts we often classify as "worse." I was bringing my own righteousness before God, weighed down by condemnation and guilt like a heavy coat. One night, as I drove to the store, the Holy Spirit spoke to me:

"Even if you didn't do it, you still aren't worthy without Me. All your righteousness is like filthy rags."

That moment was humbling. I realized that my own works and efforts, no matter how well-intentioned, could never make me righteous. Only Christ can do that. It is His righteousness that clothes us—not our works, not our "right" actions.

Ephesians 2:8-9

"For it is by grace you have been saved, through faith—and this is not from yourselves, it is the gift of God—not by works, so that no one can boast."

We are the righteousness of God **in Christ.** We have right standing with God **through Christ.** Thank God for the blood of Jesus that saved and redeemed us from the law of sin and death. This truth sets us free from being prisoners to sin.

Joel 3:10

"Let the weak say, I am strong."

It is in our weakness that God's strength is made perfect. This is when God stands up in us and flexes His power over the enemy. Greater is He that is in us than he that is in the world.

Your weakness does not define who you are.

Every hero of faith in the Bible had a weakness—Moses, David, Gideon, Rahab, Paul, and so many more. Yet God counted them righteous because of their obedience and their willingness to repent and turn back to Him. Holiness isn't just about works; it's about the posture of your heart and your obedience to God in daily life.

Again, my weakness freed me. I don't like who I am without Jesus. I need Him. My weakness became God's opportunity to show His strength in me.

The thorn is a reminder—to keep us humble, to remind us of who we truly are without God. I often pray, "Father, always keep before me who I am without You." It's a tough prayer, but it's one that invites chastening and perfection. It forces me to face myself, not to point the finger at others.

Hebrews 12:6-8

"Because the Lord disciplines the one He loves, and He chastens everyone He accepts as His son. Endure hardship as discipline; God is treating you as His children. For what children are not disciplined by their father? If you are not disciplined—and everyone undergoes discipline—then you are not legitimate, not true sons and daughters at all."

FLASHBACK

One night, the Lord chastised me and revealed the condition of my heart. I immediately recognized areas I needed to work on. In my usual theatrics, I wanted to throw myself on the floor, crying, "I'm not worthy! I'm such a terrible person!" I meant every word.

But the Holy Spirit, in His kindness, said to me, "I'm not showing you this to hurt you but to perfect you."

I am learning to boast in my infirmities, to loosen the hold of the enemy in my process of being perfected. When I confess, "I am weak," it disarms the enemy. He can't bully me with fear, doubt, insecurity, condemnation, or any other tactic.

Romans 8:1-4

"Therefore, there is now no condemnation for those who are in Christ Jesus, because through Christ Jesus the law of the Spirit who gives life has set you free from the law of sin and death."

2 Corinthians 5:17

"If anyone is in Christ, he is a new creation; old things have passed away; behold, all things have become new."

With the Holy Spirit, I am not a slave to the law of sin. I have a Redeemer and Savior who loves me and has already set me free. I expose myself before God, laying myself bare because I know where my help and strength come from.

2 Corinthians 12:8-10

"Three times I pleaded with the Lord to take it away from me. But He said to me, 'My grace is sufficient for you, for My power is made perfect in weakness.' Therefore, I will boast all the more gladly about my weaknesses, so that Christ's power may rest on me."

Paul prayed three times for God to remove the thorn in his flesh, and God's only response was, "My grace is sufficient." His grace was enough—greater than any weakness Paul faced.

How many of us have been like Paul?

We've asked God to take away a struggle, a thorn, or a weakness—the very thing that keeps us humble and dependent on Him. That thorn keeps us running **to** God and into His presence.

TRUTH IS

The Lord won't always take the thorn away. Yes, we will overcome, grow, and mature in our weaknesses throughout our lives, but the thorn often remains as a continual reminder of our dependence on Him. It serves as a testimony that God is our perpetual Savior and Deliverer. This keeps us from boasting in ourselves.

I also believe the thorn exists to help us develop the compassion of Christ. We must be touched by the infirmities of others to reach them effectively, disciple them, and love them as Christ does—even if we've never personally experienced their struggles.

Hebrews 4:15

"For we do not have a high priest who is unable to empathize with our weaknesses, but we have one who has been tempted in every way, just as we are—yet He did not sin."

LETTER 4 | MY THORN IS MY SALVATION

THERE IS SAFETY IN ACCOUNTABILITY

Over the past few years, as I've walked this healing journey with the Holy Spirit and my accountability partners, I've experienced a freedom like no other—freedom in my heart, mind, soul, and spirit. This freedom also translates into how I use my gifts and talents for His glory.

Healing and growth don't always feel good—they're often painful—but the reward is worth it. God's grace on your life makes what you do look effortless to others. But remember: it's not you. It's not me. It's **God's ability** working through us.

I encourage you to confess your faults to God and to trusted, Christ-centered accountability partners. These confidants should be integral, wise counselors with whom you can be transparent and vulnerable. My accountability partners are not "yes" people. They tell me the truth in love and grace. They hold my words in confidence and don't condemn me. Even when their corrections sting, I humble myself and say, "Yes, Lord, You're right," or simply, "Ouch, I'll do better."

Your accountability partners should pray for you, intercede on your behalf, and correct you with the spirit of love.

James 5:16

"Confess your faults to one another and pray for one another, so that you may be healed. The prayer of a righteous person is powerful and effective."

MY THORN IS MY SALVATION

My thorn keeps me at the feet of my Father. It keeps me crying out to love as He loves and in constant pursuit of needing Him above all else. Boasting in your weakness is not an excuse for arrogance or pride, but it is a reminder to bring your struggles before God. Your thorn should inspire prayer, intercession, and compassion for others.

My weakness became the sacrifice God wanted from me. It's painful, but it is where the anointing is produced. Through daily dying to ourselves and surrendering our way for His way, we find strength. Even when we fall short, we can pick ourselves up and run to Jesus for mercy and grace.

Don't hide behind your strength or your abilities. Bring God the part of you that needs to be corrected, healed, and made whole. God looks for people who need Him. He cannot fill what is already full. When we remain in a state of emptiness, we give Him room to fill us continually.

When we surrender our weaknesses to God, He is glorified in our imperfect but willing lives. Then, when He chooses to use us, we can truly say, "To God be ALL the glory."

THE HOLY INVITATION

God desires sincerity in our innermost being. When we invite the Holy Spirit into our broken places, we experience freedom, deeper fellowship with Christ, and a greater understanding of His Word and love. This vertical relationship transforms us, making us living epistles that reflect Him to the world—even without words.

Every day, there is a holy invitation to commune with the Holy Spirit, to draw nearer to God, and to receive His mercy and grace. The Father bids us to come:

Matthew 14:22-23

> *"Immediately Jesus made the disciples get into the boat and go on ahead of Him to the other side, while He dismissed the crowd. After He had dismissed them, He went up on a mountainside by Himself to pray."*

This invitation calls us to empty ourselves of selfishness and be filled with His love, character, and grace. In His presence, there is fullness of joy.

LETTER 4 | MY THORN IS MY SALVATION

Psalm 16:11

"You make known to me the path of life; You will fill me with joy in Your presence, with eternal pleasures at Your right hand."

May we become more aware of the daily invitation to draw near to Him. Our response to this invitation leads to freedom, wholeness, and a deeper connection with our Heavenly Father.

Revelation 3:20

"Behold, I stand at the door and knock. If anyone hears My voice and opens the door, I will come in and eat with him, and he with Me."

Your thorn is not a burden—it's an opportunity for God's grace to shine. Let's embrace the invitation to continually lean into His presence, allowing Him to perfect and strengthen us. He loves us deeply, and His grace is always sufficient.

LETTER 5 | MY CREATIVITY IS POWERED BY ELOHIM

LETTER 5 | MY CREATIVITY IS POWERED BY ELOHIM

"Master, Strong One, The Creator"

Genesis 1:1-3

"In the beginning God (Elohim) created the heavens and the earth. Now the earth was formless and empty, darkness was over the surface of the deep, and the Spirit of God was hovering over the waters. And God said, 'Let there be light,' and there was light. God saw that the light was good, and He separated the light from the darkness. God called the light 'day,' and the darkness He called 'night.' And there was evening, and there was morning—the first day."

The Hebrew word for God is **Elohim**—Creator God. While the word *Elohim* is plural, it is often used with a singular meaning. Elohim, the Creator, formed everything, and we are His creation.

Acts 17:28

"For in Him we live and move and have our being, as also some of your own poets have said, 'For we are also His offspring."

Everything that I am is found in Him. Elohim is the source and power of my creativity. Apart from Him, I can do nothing. But with Him, I can do all things, because He is in me, and I am in Him. I create with Father God. Through Christ, as a joint heir seated in heavenly places, I have access to divine creativity.

Our gifts and talents are **powered by God.** He anoints our hands, mouths, and minds to create. Just as transmission lines carry electrical energy from one point to another in an electric power system, connecting and distributing energy from a power source, we too function when connected to God—the **Creative Power Source** of our lives. When we are aligned with Him, His power flows through us, producing evidence and fruit—not just in one area but across every aspect of our lives.

As sons and daughters of God, we have access to the **Ultimate Source of Creativity.** However, we must understand our Creator—His character, qualities, promises, and purpose. Knowing Elohim through relationship, knowledge, and understanding gives us the authority and rights to operate as He designed us. Elohim, our Creator, who formed the sun, moon, stars, galaxies, worlds, heaven, earth, and every living creature, also influences the technologies of our age—cell phones, vehicles, quantum computing, and social media.

While God inspires and sways creation, the enemy often seeks to taint and pervert pure designs. The enemy is not a creator but an imitator. Whether acknowledged or not, creation depends on God as the source of its evolution and existence.

Everything from God is good, significant, purposeful, and intentional.

THE FRUIT OF OUR WORDS

John 1:1, 14

> *"In the beginning was the Word, and the Word was with God, and the Word was God. The same was in the beginning with God. All things were made by Him; and without Him was not anything made that was made. In Him was life; and the life was the light of men."*

> *"And the Word was made flesh, and dwelt among us, (and we beheld His glory, the glory as of the only begotten of the Father,) full of grace and truth."*

Our **words** and **thoughts** create our reality. They shape the world around us.

LETTER 5 | MY CREATIVITY IS POWERED BY ELOHIM

Proverbs 23:7

"For as he thinketh in his heart, so is he."

Our mind is like soil, and when we think (mull, digest, marinate) on negative or positive thoughts, they are like seeds being planted, rooted in the mind, and producing fruit (evidence).

We are the evidence of what we think and speak over ourselves, our situations, and our destiny.

SELF REFLECTION | What's in your heart? Is there any deception stuck in the eyes of your heart? What words are you speaking? What is the quality of your thought life? How are the words and thoughts you speak creating your reality?

Our words, our tongue, and our thoughts are a spiritual weapon. They have the power to build up or tear down, to edify or misguide, to heal or break.

Proverbs 18:21

"Death and life are in the power of the tongue, and those who love it will eat its fruit."

Proverbs 6:2

"You are snared by the words of your mouth; you are taken by the words of your mouth."

We eat the quality of fruit produced by what we speak. In the words of my spiritual mentor, "We must watch our mouths."

Our thought life is imperative. As co-creators, we are always creating with our thoughts and words. The mind is where creation, goals, and dreams begin—it starts with a thought. The enemy knows that if he can keep us in strongholds in the mind, entangled in our emotions and negative thinking, it will delay creative productivity. Thinking unhealthy thoughts affects our emotions, and our emotions reflect in our actions.

2 Corinthians 10:5

"Cast down imaginations, and every high thing that exalts itself against the knowledge of God, and bring every thought into captivity to the obedience of Christ."

We must train our minds and words with and by the Word of God as our antidote and artillery, taking dominion and authority over our thought life and word life. The battleground, the warfare, is in the spirit of the mind. If the enemy can ensnare the mind, he has our creativity, movement, and faith (action).

The renewing of the mind is necessary; it is a shedding off, a putting off, and a putting on of the new. The mind is where we are transformed from the inside out. We must ask the Father daily for the mind of Christ.

Ephesians 4:23-24

"And be continually renewed in the spirit of your mind [having a fresh, untarnished mental and spiritual attitude], ^{24} and put on the new self [the regenerated and renewed nature], created in God's image, [godlike] in the righteousness and holiness of the truth [living in a way that expresses to God your gratitude for your salvation]."

CREATION IS INSIDE OF YOU

I need you to know that what's important is what God placed inside of you and me. It's something so powerful that if we learn to **use** it, we will gain access to the creative spiritual realm. Isn't it beautiful that we get to share a piece of His glory within our lives? We are co-creators—this is our original design; this is our genesis. Your gift and talent are powered by God. We were born to give Him glory, to bring Him glory, for His glory. God (Elohim) takes delight in interacting and creating with His creation. {*Genesis 1:26-28}*

LETTER 5 | MY CREATIVITY IS POWERED BY ELOHIM

Colossians 1:16-17

"For in him all things were created: things in heaven and on earth, visible and invisible, whether thrones or powers or rulers or authorities; all things have been created through him and for him."

We are vessels of honor and worship, reflecting His heart and the Kingdom of God—for the Kingdom of God is within us. When you really think about that, what an honor and privilege it is to serve, to be chosen to serve the Kingdom of God.

It reminds me of how soldiers in the military count it an honor to serve and lay down their lives for their nation, their country, and their commander. They show complete loyalty and allegiance to their country. This mirrors how we should serve and posture our hearts before our Sovereign Lord and King—Yahweh, our holy commander. We should count it an honor and privilege to serve, giving our full allegiance to the Kingdom of God.

As Kingdom ambassadors and children, we get to **boldly** create with God. We partner with the Holy Spirit and actively participate in fulfilling God's purpose through our gifts, talents, and lives. When you think about our gifts and talents, it's not about us or for us—it is solely to bring Him glory.

Dear creative and believer, please understand this: beyond any gift or talent, we are worshippers **first.**

John 4:24

"God is Spirit, and those who worship Him must worship in Spirit and truth."

Through our gifts and talents, we function as intercessors, prayer warriors, administrators, teachers, pastors, and glory carriers. When our gifts and talents are powered by God through the Holy Spirit, we bring unseen concepts and inspirations into the natural world.

Beyond the Gift

Romans 4:17

"As it is written: 'I have made you a father of many nations.' He is our father in the sight of God, in whom he believed—the God who gives life to the dead and calls into being things that were not."

You hold something so special and rare inside of you that it cannot be duplicated. Even if someone tries to copy it, they cannot replicate **spirit**—that is God-given. This is why the Father admonishes us not to compare our gifts and talents with anyone else. There is only one **you.**

2 Corinthians 10:12

"When they measure themselves by themselves and compare themselves with themselves, they are not wise."

One of the major keys to being effective as a creative and a believer is cultivating a pure and sincere relationship with the Holy Spirit. Our prayer and faith life are the source of all things. It is crucial to be where God is—aligned in location and position—because fellowship and friendship with the Holy Spirit posture our hearts to align with His heart. In this intimacy, our desires align with His desires. In this state, we are anointed to have His eyes, His ears, and His heart, which will express through the service of our gifts, talents, and works.

Pure Hearts. Pure Hands.

The Word of the Lord says:

Psalm 24:3-6

"Who shall ascend into the hill of the Lord? Or who shall stand in his holy place? He that hath clean hands, and a pure heart; who hath not lifted up his soul unto vanity, nor sworn deceitfully. He shall receive the blessing from the Lord, and righteousness from the God of his salvation. This is the generation of them that seek him, that seek thy face, O Jacob. Selah."

LETTER 5 | MY CREATIVITY IS POWERED BY ELOHIM

Take the Limits Off

God is not limited. It's time to take the limits off—off of God and off of ourselves—because we serve a limitless God. Heaven is within you. You are limitless. Let that sink in.

I admonish you to never become settled, common, or familiar with how God uses you or wants to use you. There is always **MORE.** You can never run out of creativity or creative oil when **Elohim** is the source. This applies to every area of our lives.

The Lord is always in the **now faith.** Yield to the stretching required to grow and soar. Come out of agreement—whether conscious or subconscious—with limiting beliefs about how you perceive yourself, your situation, and your destiny. You are designed to be unfathomably **LIMITLESS.**

Ephesians 1:18-19

"I pray that the eyes of your heart may be enlightened in order that you may know the hope to which He has called you, the riches of His glorious inheritance in His holy people, and His incomparably great power for us who believe. That power is the same as the mighty strength."

My prayer is that the Holy Spirit will remove the veil from your eyes so that you may see what Abba Father has placed so uniquely and specially **inside of you.** Yes, the gift is powered by Elohim, but there is always something we must do to activate that power: we must **yield and obey.**

As Kingdom Creatives and believers, we must live in the presence of God. We must abide in Him to remain in Him.

John 15:1-5

"I am the true vine, and my Father is the gardener. He cuts off every branch in me that bears no fruit, while every branch that does bear fruit He prunes so that it will be even more fruitful. You are already

clean because of the word I have spoken to you. Remain in me, as I also remain in you. No branch can bear fruit by itself; it must remain in the vine. Neither can you bear fruit unless you remain in me. I am the vine; you are the branches. If you remain in me and I in you, you will bear much fruit; apart from me you can do nothing."

LETTER 6 | THE VALUE OF THE ONE | PARABLE OF THE TALENTS

SELF REFLECTION

LETTER 6 | THE VALUE OF THE ONE | PARABLE OF THE TALENTS

LETTER 6 | THE VALUE OF THE ONE | PARABLE OF THE TALENTS

Don't bury your gift in the ground.

God is looking for a people who will be faithful and trustworthy with the things He has placed and entrusted inside of them. Our gifts and talents are a reflection of God, distributed in the earth. They are pieces of God's likeness on display. God is so extensive, boundless, and vast that He had to deposit parts of Himself in each of us—billions of people—so His purposes and agendas could be fulfilled. That's mind-blowing.

He needs vessels for His purpose to be accomplished. In the Parable of the Talents, God gave one servant five talents, another two talents, and another one talent—each according to their own ability. God knows your design and created you uniquely. Within your God-given ability, there is a built-in measure of faith, a unique grace, and a significance that no one else has, setting you apart for your extraordinary divine purpose.

God's Investment

We are God's investment, and He ultimately desires a return on what He has placed inside of us. In various translations of the Parable of the Talents, the "talents" are referenced as gold or investments. It dawned on me that what's inside of you is **wealth**. Wealth is in your hands. We are to use what we've been given for God's purpose.

In the parable, the servants with five and two talents went out with optimism, put their talents to work, and multiplied them. It pleases the Lord to see His creation doing His will—taking dominion and authority in the areas He has called them to. This is operating in our original design. When we partner with God, we bring His vision for the earth into reality.

However, the servant with one talent went off, dug a hole, and buried his master's gift. When the master returned and asked for an account of his investment, the servant with one talent made excuses: "I was afraid and hid your gift in the ground," or, "I was afraid to lose the talent," or even, "I was afraid I might disappoint you, so I carefully buried your gift."

This servant counted himself out before he even started. What's striking in the parable is that no enemy influenced him to bury his gift. He allowed fear, self-doubt, and negative thinking to overtake him, preventing him from even attempting to obey.

Self-Reflection

What fear is making you bury your gift or talent?

Is it fear of failure? Fear of success? Fear of the unknown? Fear of _____? Write it down.

Don't allow fear to make you forfeit your destiny, your purpose, and the promises of God that already belong to you. Don't let the enemy deceive you with lies about who you are or your God-given ability.

BACK TO THE PARABLE

The master was furious with the servant's excuses and lack of effort. He called him a "lazy and wicked" servant, saying, "It's criminal to cautiously live like that—to play it safe and live in inequity." Knowing what to do and refusing to do it is deliberate disobedience.

In the parable, the one talent was taken from the servant and given to the one who had five talents and multiplied them. The servant with one talent was cast into outer darkness.

LETTER 6 | THE VALUE OF THE ONE | PARABLE OF THE TALENTS

God desires us to partner with Him in His purposes. It is an honor and privilege to serve as His Kingdom representatives. But let us not forget to reverence God's perfect sovereignty. When we fail to value what He has placed in us, His purpose will still be accomplished—with or without us. God has a holy agenda in the Kingdom of Heaven that **will** be fulfilled.

Dear Creative Believer,

Do not ignore or disregard the blessing and gift God has placed inside you. We are His investment. Value what He has entrusted to you.

Matthew 25:29

"For to everyone who has [and values his blessings and gifts from God, and has used them wisely], more will be given, and [he will be richly supplied so that] he will have an abundance; but from the one who does not have [because he has ignored or disregarded his blessings and gifts from God], even what he does have will be taken away."

Comparison and fear kill authenticity, creativity, and purpose. We don't need to look outside ourselves for what God has already placed within us. The one talent is just as valuable as the five and two talents. We must give God back His investment. We must cultivate, steward, and faithfully manage what He has given us.

Remember: We are never owners, only managers. Everything that God created in you and for you is **GOOD.** We insult God when we look outside of ourselves, compare our gifts, or allow the spirit of fear and unbelief to stagnate us from moving in His faith and courage for the things He has called us to.

Joshua 1:9

"Have I not commanded you? Be strong and courageous. Do not be afraid; do not be discouraged, for the Lord your God will be with you wherever you go."

You are fearfully and wonderfully made. Think about it—why did God use the word **"fearfully"**? By inspiration, the Lord was so meticulous when He created us, so "fearfully" means carefully, ensuring no mistakes. Everything about you is intentional, purposeful, and **GOOD**.

We must come into agreement with our Heavenly Father concerning our divine identity in Christ and the purpose over our lives. Come into agreement that He thought of you and me to partner with Him in His **master plan** to save, deliver, and redeem this world. We are His workmanship.

Ephesians 2:10

"For we are God's handiwork, created in Christ Jesus to do good works, which God prepared in advance for us to do."

You were created to do marvelous and good works in the earth. Yes, **YOU**. These good works are already prepared—set, charted, and customized for you to accomplish.

The Lord knows how much we can handle and steward. It's not about the size or the number. Don't be deceived. If God told you to steward 50, 100, or 5,000 people, that's what **He** told you to do. Let's not get caught up in the standards and values of this fractured, failing, and falling world system or its measures of success.

Your gift has value. You are **NEEDED.** You are **SIGNIFICANT.** The world needs your voice, your sound, and your creations. There are people assigned to your **YES** and your call. God is counting on you! He has placed an investment in you.

Creative, believer, son, daughter—take your gift out of the ground, or don't settle in the gifts and talents you've already perfected; **THERE IS MORE.** Start working the gift God has given you simply by obeying the first thing He told you to do.

"Write the vision, make it plain, and run with it." (*Habakkuk 2:2*).

LETTER 6 | THE VALUE OF THE ONE | PARABLE OF THE TALENTS

May He stir up the gifts inside of you in Jesus' name. Once He reveals and anoints—**OBEY.** Don't focus on what you don't have. We serve a God who makes **something out of nothing.** The impossible (**I'm possible**) is His specialty.

Don't allow the enemy to use you or unhealed areas of your life to make you forfeit your purpose and destiny. The enemy does not have the power to **stop** us. However, we can become the weapon that is formed against ourselves.

John 10:10

"The thief comes only to steal and kill and destroy; I have come that they may have life, and have it to the full."

The enemy is on a relentless mission to kill, steal, and destroy **purpose and destiny.**

Empty the Grave

As creatives and believers, we cannot live in the emotional realm. We must arise in the confidence of God and in our identity in Him.

The grave is full of untapped potential and buried gifts. Don't die full of dreams, aspirations, wealth, and treasure trapped inside of you—things you never poured out into the earth.

We must leave this earth **empty, not full.**

LETTER 7 | Identity: I AM | The Higher Calling to Sonship

LETTER 7 | Identity: I AM | The Higher Calling to Sonship

Genesis 1:27

"So God created man in His own image; in the image of God He created him."

The **I AM** lives inside of you. You were created in the image and likeness of God. That is your origin; that is your genesis. Your biological parents were the vessel that brought you into the earthly realm, but your **true identity**—your **divine DNA**—is in your Heavenly Father. You were designed in the beautiful mind of God: the **"I AM that I AM."**

From the beginning, God charged us to:

"Be fruitful and multiply; fill the earth and subdue it; have dominion over the fish of the sea, over the birds of the air, and over every living thing that moves on the earth." (*Genesis 1:28*).

We were created to procreate, to speak things into existence, and to have dominion. "We have keys to the Kingdom of Heaven, and whatever we bind on earth shall be bound in heaven, and whatever we loose on earth shall be loosed in heaven." This is the power God has given us through Christ Jesus as joint heirs.

God has bestowed on us spiritual birthrights, benefits, privileges, limited powers, and authority as His sons and daughters.

So, how do we create? The first thing that comes to mind is the **mind** itself—through the power of our thoughts, imagination, and words. Our words produce our physical reality.

Our words are **life and death.**

"I AM" statements are profoundly powerful. They are directly tied to God-like declarations because God **IS.** He is the **"I AM THAT I AM."** When we call on the **"I AM,"** we are calling God by His name.

So, when we say things like:

- "I'm (I AM) broke."
- "I'm (I AM) not enough."
- "I'm (I AM) always lonely."
- "I'm (I AM) always tired."
- "I'm (I AM) afraid."

We are creating our reality with those words, fixing them as truth in our lives—especially when we don't replace them with words of faith and truth from the Word of God. We bind our identity to the words we create.

Now imagine if we replaced those faithless "I AM" statements with **faith-filled declarations**:

- "I AM more than enough."
- "I AM blessed to be a blessing."
- "I AM never alone."
- "I AM never in lack."

God has given us the legal rights to speak into the spiritual realm where He abides, and where He hears our words spoken into the atmosphere.

Let's be clear: We all have moments when our words and faith are shaken, and discouragement creeps in. This is not about self-denial—it's human to feel this way. However, it is critical to watch what we say and release into the atmosphere, even in distress or anger, because the enemy is the **"prince of the air."** His advantage lies in our words and vulnerabilities.

We must continually guard our mouths and train our faith muscles to remain vigilant. While it's normal to feel emotions, we must not stay in those emotional moments too long, because our words are always creating.

LETTER 7 | Identity: I AM | The Higher Calling to Sonship

Joint Heirs

Psalm 82:6

"You are gods, and all of you are children of the Most High."

Ephesians 2:6

"And God raised us up with Christ and seated us with him in the heavenly realms in Christ Jesus."

I've been an educator in the school system for about a decade. I taught English for two years, and I love words. Looking into the **-ed** suffix, it means past, present, and future. It also signifies something done, finished, or complete. So, when God says we are "seated" with Christ, it is a **finished work**—it's complete.

We have more power and authority than we often operate in through Him. One of the enemy's greatest tricks lies in the war grounds of the mind. Spiritually, the fiery darts of the enemy are like arrows targeting and ambushing our thoughts. The battle over our thought life—limiting beliefs about ourselves formed by past experiences, failures, disappointments, pain, grief, or offense—can mask our God-given identity.

Let me repeat: **the enemy can't stop destiny and purpose, but he can send delays or deceptions** to keep us from fully tapping into our **identity: I AM.**

Our warfare is not with people. Our adversary is not flesh and blood. The enemy is after one thing: **identity.** In our identity lies our purpose, destiny, authority, access, and the full rights to the Kingdom of God that belong to us through Christ Jesus.

2 Corinthians 10:4-6

"For the weapons of our warfare are not carnal but mighty in God for pulling down strongholds, casting down arguments and every

high thing that exalts itself against the knowledge of God, bringing every thought into captivity to the obedience of Christ, and being ready to punish all disobedience when your obedience is fulfilled."

THE SPIRIT OF SONSHIP

It is time to **arise and shine** in the spirit of our minds as the Father's children, embracing the Spirit of Sonship. There is an urgency for sonship in the Body of Christ. The Spirit of Sonship is crucial and necessary to our **Identity: I AM.**

There are **benefits** for those who ascend and grow in sonship within the Kingdom of God.

"Who shall ascend the mountain of the Lord? Or who shall stand in His holy place? He that has clean hands and a pure heart."

Breaking down the terms **benefits** and **ascend:**

In a natural sense, benefits refer to advantage, satisfaction, enjoyment, strength, and blessing. To ascend means to soar, arise, and mount up. Spiritually, this means there is **advantage, satisfaction, enjoyment, strength, and blessing** in the Kingdom of God when we arise and mount up in sonship.

What Is Sonship?

Galatians 4:6-7

"Because you are his sons, God sent the Spirit of His Son into our hearts, the Spirit who calls out, 'Abba, Father.'"

The Spirit of Sonship is a heart of servitude unto the Lord. True sonship is a posture, an attitude, and a covenant relationship.

Sonship is to **know the will of the Father** and to **do the will of the Father.** It is working in concert, joined with God, to fulfill His purpose on earth. In the Spirit of Sonship, there is identity, authority, dominion, power, inheritance, and fellowship with God.

LETTER 7 | Identity: I AM | The Higher Calling to Sonship

Sonship requires submission to the will of the Father. It is the heart posture of saying, "Not my will, but Your will, Lord." In sonship, we grow with God and live in Him, knowing our identity in Christ, our rightful place, and functioning in it.

It is having the same attitude as Christ—the heart of a son fully aligned with the will of the Father.

Jesus is the ultimate model and pattern of sonship.

In the Bible, we also see examples of the Spirit of Sonship in figures like **Elisha** and **Esther.** Their servitude and submission qualified them for sonship, enabling them to receive mantles and promotions.

Focusing on Jesus, we see how, as a son, He was fully submitted to the will of the Father. Jesus only did what the Father told Him to do. His authority flowed directly from His identity as a son.

Sonship is the foundation for Kingdom authority.

Here's my favorite part: sonship is about relationship with Abba more than works, performance, or ministry. **God wants relationship over works.**

In sonship, we draw strength from relationship, communion, and worship. We cannot become so busy doing things for God that we forget to simply **be** with the Giver of the gifts. This is the heartbeat of sonship.

It's not complex. It's all about **relationship.**

Our Heavenly Father **wants us** and yearns for deeper fellowship with us. This is essential so that the Holy Spirit can reveal areas in us that need to be perfected and aligned—our hearts to His heart, our thoughts to His thoughts, and our ways to His ways. In sonship, we **must** be perfected. This involves breaking, crushing, pressing, and molding our will and character to reflect His.

Sonship is about submission and obedience—not out of obligation, but because we **love** Him. In sonship, everything is **Kingdom-driven.** It always points back to the will of the Father.

Sonship means embracing correction, having a teachable spirit, and maintaining the right attitude and perspective. The Father chastens those He loves, and His love perfects us. This perfection often comes through leadership—pastors, teachers, and others after God's own heart—who we should submit to as delegated, integral authorities.

Sonship requires sticking with God, being faithful and committed beyond our own will and way. Even when the warfare intensifies, we cannot retreat, run, or hide from God or the call. Instead, we must remain loyal to our Heavenly Father. As sons and daughters of the Most High God, we must choose not to turn back on our sonship.

Luke 9:62

"Jesus said, 'No one who puts a hand to the plow and looks back is fit for service in the Kingdom of God.'"

It's time to run to God—the God of mercy and grace—and pick up the assignment you may have dropped or buried. **You are needed in this hour.** The Kingdom of God is at hand. Repent, turn to Him, and He will heal your land. That is His promise. God is bringing us back into alignment with the Spirit of Sonship.

The Enemy's Agenda

The enemy doesn't want the children of God to step into the benefits of the Kingdom that are available to those who arise and soar into sonship. These benefits include a divine identity—not as the world gives—but one that carries authority, dominion, and power.

The enemy seeks to keep us in partial obedience, preventing us from receiving the fullness of the Kingdom benefits that belong to us as joint heirs with Christ. Satan is furious because, through Jesus' sacrifice on Calvary, we have been reinstated as co-heirs.

LETTER 7 | Identity: I AM | The Higher Calling to Sonship

Thank You, Jesus, for the blood that paid the price in full!

Let us take our rightful place, Body of Christ!

This statement is so **POWERFUL:**
"The degree to which we respond and answer the will and instructions of God determines how much force and power of the Kingdom will operate in our lives to make our destiny a reality."

Your **YES** is the **KEY.**

Benefits of Growing and Arising in Sonship

- **Identity**: Not as the world gives, but identity in spirit and truth (revelation, realization, and actualization).
- **Authority, Boldness, and Confidence**: The ability to go to God without hesitation.
- **Heirs of the Promise**: Co-heirs, seated with Christ in heavenly places.
- **Keys to the Kingdom of Heaven**: To bind and loose.
- **Dominion and Access**: Direct entrance into God's purpose and the ability to decree a thing and see it established.
- **Clothed and United with Christ**: A reflection of Him.
- **Freedom from Sin**: No longer a slave to sin, but living in the freedom of Christ.
- **A New Life in Heavenly Realms**: Operating in the **4th dimension**, the heavenly realms.
- **Abundance - Natural and Spiritual Wealth** { Ephesians 3:20-21 , Matthew 6:33}

The ultimate benefit is the purpose of our existence. On **that day**, as sons and daughters walking in the Spirit of Sonship, we will hear:

"Well done, good and faithful servant. Enter the joy of the Lord."

This is our pursuit. This is the higher calling. Fellowship with and obedience to Abba Father is what we are called to fulfill on earth.

"People will know you based on what you do in the earth, but God ONLY knows you and me for our relationship with HIM. God only knows us according to the way we KNOW Him."

~ CeCe Winans

LETTER 8| "I AM" Embodied Rhema Declaration

LETTER 8 | "I AM" Embodied Rhema Declaration

(Add movement to your declaration)

I AM _____ **(an affirming characteristic)**

I AM _____ **(an affirming characteristic)**

I AM PURPOSED TO

_____

I WILL NOT ALLOW

_____

I AM PURPOSED TO BE

_____

MY IDENTITY IS ROOTED IN CHRIST JESUS.

So, I AM MORE THAN

_____

LETTER 8| "I AM" Embodied Rhema Declaration

I AM _____ (repeat affirming characteristic from above)

I AM _____ (repeat affirming characteristic from above)

"For I know the plans I have for you," declares the LORD, "plans to prosper you and not to harm you, plans to give you hope and a future." ~ Jeremiah 29:11

Beyond the Gift

LETTER 9 | "I ASCEND" Embodied Rhema Declaration

LETTER 9 | "I ASCEND" Embodied Rhema Declaration

(Read aloud and declare / Add movement to your declaration)

I Ascend

I Ascend beyond _____ *(what's weighing you down emotionally)*

I Mount up beyond _____ *(what's weighing you down emotionally)*

I ... Ascend

Tearing down _____

And dying to _____

"For He raised us from the dead along with Christ and seated us with Him in the heavenly realms."

So, I Arise in _____

(what do you want to arise in)

LETTER 9 | "I ASCEND" Embodied Rhema Declaration

I Soar in _____

(what do you want to soar in)

I Ascend.

Beyond the Gift

LETTER 10 | "BE HEALED"

LETTER 10 | "BE HEALED"

SELF REFLECTION

What was the root that makes you feel that you weren't (loved, enough, accepted, validated, protected etc.):

_____

_____

_____

_____

What happened? What said? (Expose it/ Identify it):

_____

_____

_____

_____

Divorce it/ uproot it:

_____

_____

_____

_____

LETTER 10 | "BE HEALED"

Replace it with the Word of God. Who does He say you are?

_____

_____

_____

_____

I AM _____ **(an affirming characteristic)**

I AM _____ **(an affirming characteristic)**

I AM _____**(an affirming characteristic)**

Beyond the Gift

ABOUT THE AUTHOR

Hope Radiance Boyd is the Founder and Director of Yahweh in Motion Dance Company of the Arts International, where they embody Isaiah 61 through the power of the arts. She has served and dedicated over a decade to empowering and mentoring creatives through arts, education, and ministry. With a deep passion for arts evangelism and wholeness within the Arts & Entertainment, Media, and Education sectors, she has established herself as a global voice in cultivating and nurturing creative gifts for the Kingdom of God.

As a Dance Instructor, Minister, Director, and Theatrical Composer, Hope travels extensively, both nationally and internationally. Her life's mission is to provide a platform for creatives believers, and humanity to uncover and their purpose and experience freedom and healing in Christ through the arts. Through her work, she seeks to illuminate the world with the saving, delivering, and redeeming power of Jesus Christ, helping individuals' step into their God-given calling and impact their communities for the Kingdom and Glory of God.

Made in the USA
Columbia, SC
11 April 2025